One teenage marriage broke up so fast they're still fighting over who gets custody of the wedding cake.

THE
JOKE IS
WILD

The Joke Is
WILD

Way-out New Humor
By
Stanley Davis

Illustrated
by Don Branham

HALLMARK EDITIONS

THE JOKE IS WILD

The President says business is good—but then he's got a better location, and he doesn't have to pay any rent.

A man went into a fancy restaurant and ordered *Poulet a la Maserati*. It turned out to be a chicken that had been run over by an Italian sports car.

The Beatles have sold 40 million records, and it's your tough luck if you happen to live next door to the teenager who bought them all.

Christopher Columbus set an example the Government's never forgotten. He didn't know where he was going, he didn't know where he was when he got there, and he did it all on borrowed money.

One recent college graduate got a job putting

makeup on chorus girls for $50 a week. That isn't much, but it was all he could afford.

The teachers don't keep the kids after school these days. When 3:30 comes, they're afraid to be alone in the same building with them.

The Government is still trying to help small business. A little fellow at the shopping center used to make the rounds with a hand organ and a monkey. The Government gave him a loan. Now he goes around with a steam calliope and a gorilla.

They're making an electric car in Detroit now that can go anywhere in the country. All you need is a 3,000-mile extension cord.

A man was explaining that he only took a drink to steady himself, when his wife put in,

"Yes, but sometimes he gets so steady he can't move for days."

A man was bragging to his wife about losing a few pounds, but she thought otherwise. "You didn't lose them," she said. "Summer's coming and they just went around in back where there's more shade."

There was a courteous teenager on the bus yesterday. He not only gave an old lady his seat, he even offered her his hair spray.

The toughest part of getting a college education these days is finding a place to park.

You can't trust an airline stewardess. They come up to you very sweetly and say, "What can I do for you?" and then strap you down in your seat.

A gourmet is a fellow who can sip a glass of wine and tell you not only what year it was bottled, but who jumped on the grapes.

A teenage girl and her mother were visiting a neighbor. When they left, the neighbor remarked on how well-behaved the girl was. "Not really," said her mother. "She's just not used to talking until she hears a dial tone."

Advertising has made the bathroom the most popular room in the house. One true believer gets up at four in the morning, goes into the bathroom, and uses every brand of deodorant, mouthwash, and toothpaste he sees on television. He doesn't want to offend. He's never offended anyone because he's never left the bathroom.

You can always tell when a marriage is shaky. The partners don't even talk to each other during television commercials.

A confirmed optimist is a fellow who gets married at 93 and then buys a house near a school.

One widower was so lazy he married his first wife's sister so he wouldn't have to break in a new mother-in-law.

Movies on planes are a growing problem. The other day a businessman was flying to New York, watching the movie, and he forgot where he was and stepped outside for popcorn.

The other passengers thought he was the added attraction.

Can you imagine anything more dated than a Cuban travel poster?

A wife attempted to convince her husband that she should buy several wigs. "Wouldn't you like to have a date with a blonde one night, a brunette the next night, and a redhead the next?"

"That's all right with me," said her husband, "but don't give me any trouble when I come home."

In Hollywood they get married in the morning. That way, if it doesn't work out you haven't wasted a whole day.

Recently a major network showed the first ultramodern Western on TV. The medicine man refused to make tepee calls.

A Chinese waiter served a customer an Italian dinner and advised the customer on all the various dishes in Italian. Later the customer asked the owner, "How come the Chinese waiter speaks Italian?"

The owner said, "Shh! he thinks he's learning English."

An Englishman complained about the strangeness of American customs. "Over here," he said, "you order hot tea, then put ice in it to make it cold, then put sugar in it to make it sweet, then put lemon in it to make it sour, then lift your glass, say 'Here's to you,' and drink it yourself."

They say you're supposed to tip the waitress at those key clubs by adding up her measurements and leaving 10 per cent.

A man put a card in one of those date-matching computers that said, "I am young, handsome, and wealthy, and I'm looking for someone to love."

Out came a card from the machine: "Don't just stand there. Kiss me."

The old millionaire and his child bride just had an anniversary. He gave her a 20-carat diamond, and she gave him the mumps.

SPARKLE
SPARKLE

TV commercial in the year 2000: A man is bragging that he smokes ten packs of cigarettes a day. His friend asks, "Do you save the coupons?"

And the man returns, "Where do you think I got this artificial heart?"

If folk singers get any younger they'll be protesting Pablum and rough diapers.

Science has made fantastic strides in the last decade—it's now only 60 years behind the comic books.

One poor fellow is so bashful he won't open an oyster unless he knocks first.

The unluckiest man in America practiced for five years forging another man's signature on checks. When he perfected the signature, signed a check and cashed it, the check came back marked "Insufficient Funds."

Grandfather says his hometown used to be 1) so strict that even the katydids didn't dare, and 2) so slow the town didn't get June bugs until nearly August.

An old-timer is a man who remembers when the only problem about parking a car was getting the girl to agree to it.

If you think you can be happy by letting the Government take care of you, just remember what happened to the American Indian.

The supermarket manager overheard a man bragging about how much he'd been stealing from the store.

The next time the man came in the man-

ager followed him around. The man loaded his cart, paid in full at the check-out counter, and put the groceries in his car. The man did this five or six times, and each time he paid the cashier. Finally the manager couldn't stand the suspense, so he went to the man and said, "Listen, I've been watching you and I've never seen you hide anything under your coat and you paid for everything you bought. What are you stealing?"

And the man said, "Shopping carts."

The famous heiress has been married so many times that she never leaves home anymore without a drip-dry wedding dress. Her wedding license is made out "To Whom It May Concern."

A new recruit worked out a great system for surviving basic training. If a thing moved, he saluted it. If it didn't move, he picked it up. If it was too heavy to pick up, he painted it. The system worked fine until one day when he painted the general's wife.

Who today remembers General Custer's famous words, "Men, don't take any prisoners"?

The trouble with the music teenagers listen to these days is that you can't tell when the record is worn out.

A rich old lady died and left her pet poodle $200,000, but the dog didn't get a cent—her parakeet sued and broke the will.

Most husbands are losing the war on poverty because their wives fraternize with the enemy.

A Texan died and went to heaven. St. Peter greeted him at the gate and asked, in a friendly kind of way, where the man was from.

"Texas," he replied.

"Well," said St. Peter, "come on in, but you aren't going to be satisfied."

When a lady driver ran out of gas, a gentleman on the sidewalk came over and offered to push her car. He pushed the car for half a mile and suddenly saw a filling station pass by and yelled, "Why didn't you turn in there?"

"I never go there," she said. "They don't give trading stamps."

America is the only country where they lock up the jury and let the prisoner go home.

Someone opened a fortune cookie in a Chinese restaurant the other day and it said "Better tip big—we've got the Bomb too."

Why are hotel walls so thin when you're trying to sleep, and so thick when you're trying to listen?

A railroad flagman was dozing on the steps of

a caboose when the trainmaster came by and stopped in front of him. Sensing trouble, the flagman raised his head, opened his eyes, and said slowly, "Amen."

There's a slot machine in Las Vegas with a sign on it that says "In case of atomic attack, hide under this crazy machine—it's never been hit yet."

There's a fortune waiting for the person who can invent a windshield wiper that won't hold parking tickets.

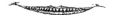

A famous actor's wife sued her husband for divorce and named his mirror as corespondent.

The way the teenagers wear their hair now, you don't give a kid a buck for a haircut, you take him to three shops and get an estimate.

TV commercials are amazing. They make it possible for an ordinary citizen in New York to see a talented actor in Hollywood suffering from acid indigestion.

The other day a teacher sneezed in school and a little girl said "God bless you," and the teacher said, "You'd better cut that out or we're both in trouble."

If you really want trouble, try asking for catsup in a Chinese restaurant.

One famous writer had a pen name, an unlisted phone, a cable address and a Swiss bank account. When he died they couldn't find him to bury him.

The government is really trying to beautify America. For example: the last time Superman flew over a city and rescued someone, he knocked over a trash can. Now the poor guy has to land at the airport like everyone else.

One good thing about being a hippie. You'll never miss an important phone call because you're in the bathtub.

The Famous Actress was embarrassed the other night at her big party. Her dressmaker had on the same dress she was wearing, and it looked better on him.

One good thing about business luncheons— they give you a chance to sober up again before the cocktail hour.

Fifty per cent of the population is now under 25. Maybe we don't need Medicare as much as we do a sure cure for diaper rash.

If the President ever wants to end a war, he should put it on television. That way it would only last 13 weeks.

If you want to get your wife home fast from a vacation, send her your local newspaper with something clipped out of it.

Teenage boys will walk ten miles in a protest parade, but when they're home they even ride their motorcycles from the bedroom to the breakfast table.

A panhandler stopped a man on the street and asked him for a dime.

"A dime won't buy anything these days," the man said. "Don't you want a quarter?"

Replied the panhandler: "No, with all the shady characters around today, I don't like to carry too much cash."

The best client a lawyer ever had is a scared millionaire.

The first thing the psychiatrist told the patient was that he'd have to give up smoking.

"Give up smoking?" said the patient. "Will that help me?"

"No," said the psychiatrist, "but you'll stop burning holes in my couch."

25

It must be wonderful to be a child. Every night you can turn on your television set and take your pick of dozens of movies you've never seen before.

A bachelor was bragging that he'd been out every evening: Monday with Edith, Tuesday with Caroline, Wednesday with Fido—and his friend stopped him and said, "Fido sounds like a dog."

The bachelor moaned. "If you think Fido's a dog, you should see Edith and Caroline."

The only way to get a doctor to make a house call any more is to marry him.

A bandit held up a gas station the other night, took every cent in the place, roared away in his car—and then roared back about three minutes later.

"You got all the money I had," said the owner. "What do you want now?"

26

Said the bandit: "I just remembered your sign said you give trading stamps."

The Government spent $3 billion to take pictures of the moon, rushed them back to earth, and then found out that the drugstore couldn't develop them until next week.

Just think, while you're sitting here reading this book, a big fat computer somewhere is checking your tax returns.

The girls are all wearing shorter skirts, and necklines are lower too. The boys don't know where it's all going to end, but they hope they're around when it does.

A famous singer is going back on television next year—the network renewed his liquor license. But in Kansas they have to sell his records under the counter. He's the only singer who records at 33 and a fifth.

Education is really a wonderful thing. After all, if you couldn't sign your name, you'd have to pay cash.

Since the invention of girdles, women now take up one third less space in the world.

A man on safari in Africa had a frightening experience. He lost his guide, wandered into the jungle, and suddenly he was surrounded by hostile natives with what looked like human bones in their hair. Then he remembered a trick he'd seen in an old movie. He scratched in his pocket for his cigarette lighter, pulled it out, flicked it once, and a big flame popped up. The natives were impressed and stood back. Then the chief spoke up: "It's a miracle," he said. "I've never seen a lighter that worked the first time."

Baseball clubs now have two teams—one for playing ball and one for shaving commercials.

A fisherman trolled all day and caught just one fish, but it was only five inches long, so he threw it back. The next day he caught another five-inch fish and threw him back. A month later he returned to the same spot. He caught a fish. It was five inches long. Just when he was about to throw it back, the fish looked up and said, "You're wasting your time, buddy. We're all midgets here."

A rock-and-roller was being treated for a wrenched knee and his first question was, "Will I still be able to sing, Doc?"

A mother was trying to lose some weight by going on liquid diet food, but she had to stop. Her little daughter went all over the neighborhood saying, "My mother doesn't eat any more, she just drinks."

It's a funny thing about cities. New York wants to get rid of its pigeons, and Las Vegas wants to get more of them.

One famous American scientist had better watch his step. The press asked him what our astronauts would be likely to find on the moon, and he said, "Russians."

A good tip for alcoholics is never drive while you're drinking. You might spill some.

One thing about a woman driver. When she sticks out her hand you can be certain she's going to turn left, turn right, back up, stop, or dry her nails.

Mixed emotions: a state of mind occasioned by seeing your mother-in-law drive off a cliff in your new car.

One family man has so many children he's afraid to go home and ask, "What's new?"

Spring is here and two bird watchers met in a park and fell in love. They're to be married next Saturday and a whippoorwill will give the bride away.

There's a rumor that Bob Hope just signed up for 13 more wars.

Nothing improves a person's driving like a police car cruising alongside.

A group of tourists were stranded on a desert island, shipwrecked and forlorn. "It's hopeless," said one. "We're lost and they'll never find us."

"Yes they will," said another. "Remember, we took this cruise on the installment plan."

If the politicians keep getting into show business, you're going to have to send for the *Congressional Record* to see which albums are in the Top Ten.

The new movies are all for adults only. If you aren't an adult when you go in, you sure are when you come out.

A politician is someone who believes you don't have to fool the people all the time. Just during election campaigns.

A man at a restaurant complained to the manager about how tough the steak was, and the manager yelled, "Get out, this is no place for weaklings!"

These days, when you see a father and son together, the one with the beard is the son.

If you can't take a trip to Europe, you can get the same effect just by staying home and tipping every other person you meet.

It was a very friendly resort. The girls were all looking for husbands, and the husbands were all looking for girls.

If you want to separate the boys from the men, just bring on the girls.

These days girls don't marry men to reform them. They want to get in on the fun themselves.

The reason the cowboy never wins the girl on television is that when a fellow rides a horse, eats with a horse, and sleeps beside a horse 24 hours a day, it's not easy for a girl to get close to him.

Abe Lincoln wouldn't have any trouble getting an education these days. He'd have been a cinch for a scholarship as a basketball center.

An old-timer is someone who remembers when a family went for a drive on Sunday afternoon and everyone got into the same car.

Talk about happy marriages. There's a couple who've been married 25 years and they still go out to dinner and dancing twice a week. She goes on Mondays and Wednesdays and he goes on Tuesdays and Thursdays.

A woman called her doctor hysterically the other day and said, "Doctor, you've got to come right over. When my husband got up he took his vitamin pill, his ulcer pill, his tranquilizer pill, his antihistamine pill, his appetite depressant pill, and his heart pill, and then he lit a cigarette. Then there was an explosion and now I can't find him."

A girl's best hobby is whatever interests the man she's interested in.

An old Indian stood at the top of a hill with his son, looking over the beautiful valley below. He mused awhile, then said, "Someday, my son, this land belong to Indian again—palefaces all go to moon."

Anyone can find a doctor these days. The caddies all have walkie-talkies.

Las Vegas has all kinds of gambling devices — roulette tables, slot machines, wedding chapels...

Have you seen the dances the kids do nowadays? They don't speak, they don't look at each other, they don't touch. They act as if they've been married 30 years.

A Texas teenager told his father he needed some oil for his hair. His father bought him Oklahoma.

An executive was complaining about the stock market: "If I bought General Motors, wagon trains would come back."

Someone ought to write a really modern Western. The big scene would feature the hero in front of the saloon trying to find a place for his horse.

Sign on a high-school fence: "Don't be a dropout. Stay in school and help us drive the teachers nuts."

Tough luck is when you reach your September years and find out you missed the best of July and August.

When a rancher complained that his boots were too tight, his friend suggested he have them stretched.

"Nothing doing," the rancher replied. "These boots are too tight and that's the way they're going to stay. Every morning I've got to get up and round up all the cattle that busted out during the night, and mend the fences they tear down, and watch my ranch blowing away in the dust, and then spend the evening listening to my wife nag me about moving to the city. When I get ready for bed and pull these tight boots off, that's the only real pleasure I get all day."

A man had a horrible nightmare. He dreamed he jumped from a plane, pulled his parachute rip cord, and the chute didn't open. Then he looked down, and waiting on the ground to catch him was an outfielder from the New York Mets.

Skirts these days come in three lengths—short, shorter, and Good Morning Judge.

Hollywood is where every year they hold the Academy Awards in Santa Monica to decide on the best picture that was made in Europe.

Some women wait so long for their dreamboat to come along that their piers collapse.

One rich couple is about to get married and neither of them can figure out whom to invite to the wedding. They've already married all their friends.

The other day a wife walked into her husband's office and found him kissing his secretary. Quick as a flash, he shouted, "Make two copies of that and send one to my wife!"

Do you realize that Fidel Castro could steal $50 million, shave his beard, and no one would ever know what he looks like?

If a lady governor and her husband should split up, who would get custody of the state?

A young man went to a psychiatrist and complained that all he could think of was food. Even in his dreams, he complained, he dreamed of nothing but food.

Said the psychiatrist: "That's funny, most boys your age dream of girls."

And the young man said, "Oh, I dream of girls too, but when I do I'm always pouring catsup on them."

When a man complained in a restaurant that he'd found a fly in his soup, the manager came running over and said, "Congratulations, all day long my waiters have been trying to catch that fly, and just imagine — you, a total stranger, have succeeded."

A lot of girls would have hourglass figures if time hadn't shifted the sands.

A television sponsor is a guy who watches the commercials and goes to the refrigerator during the show.

The government has finally solved the housing problem for veterans. They call it re-enlistment.

You have to be smart to get along these days. One bright guy wore a mask all his life so nobody could recognize him. He only took it off when he was robbing a bank.

The big thing now is split-level homes. Thirty years ago if you lived over a garage you kept quiet about it.

Most people would be glad to attend to their own business if the Government would just give it back to them.

A kid who had never seen anything but TV was taken to a movie for the first time. When the movie came on the screen he crowed, "Wow! What reception!"

People who live in glass houses shouldn't throw parties.

How about those astronauts. They crawl into a crowded capsule, fly into millions of miles of uncharted space, get out and walk around with nothing under them for 150 miles, parachute to earth from 50,000 feet—and then have to light a cigarette from a package that says, "Caution: Cigarette Smoking May Be Hazardous to Your Health."

"Dad, I've got my first part in a play," said the young would-be actor. "I play a man who's been married 20 years."

"That's fine, son," replied the father. "Next time you might even get a speaking part."

The new cars are really powerful. They've got power brakes, power steering, power windows, power antennas—there's so much power, you don't drive the car, you just sit there and tremble.

They say a dollar doesn't go very far these days, but that's not so. It goes all the way to Washington.

A woman came into a police station to report her husband missing and described him as "29 years old, 6 feet 3 inches tall, blond and handsome."

"I knew your husband," said the desk sergeant. "He was bald, fat, and 40."

"I know," the woman said, "and who wants *him* back?"

Did you ever notice that when a family is fighting to keep the wolf from the door, the stork usually comes down the chimney?

47

There's a new car on the market that won't solve the safety problem but may save the owner money. It's painted red on one side and yellow on the other. If you have an accident all the witnesses contradict each other.

The big trouble with the bucket seats on to-day's sporty cars is that everyone doesn't have the same size bucket.

He wouldn't say how old he was, but his Social Security card is number 3.

The two old fishermen were sitting on the bridge with their lines in the water, and to make things more interesting they bet on who would catch the first fish. Then one of them got so excited he fell off the bridge into the river.

"Consarn!" yelled the other down to the water. "If you're going to *dive* for them, Clem, the bet's off!"

A lady social worker visited the local jail. She asked a dejected man in one cell, "Was it your love of liquor that brought you here?"

"Gosh no, lady," he answered. "You can't get nothing in here."

Girl coping with an obnoxious blind date at a party: "You seem like such a marvelous, interesting, considerate, intelligent person. What other imitations do you do?"

An impatient fisherman tried five different kinds of bait without success, even though he could see the fish through the clear water. Disgusted, he reeled in his line, reached into his pocket, and tossed a handful of change into the water. "Go on, then," he yelled. "Buy something you *do* like!"

The first lesson a baby learns at its mother's knees in these modern times is to be careful of her stockings.

Two stern-faced Maine men went fishing one day in an old boat. For three hours neither of them moved a muscle. Then the one aft got restless. "Doggone it, Abe," said the other, "that's the third time you've shuffled your feet

in an hour. You come out here to fish or prac-
tice dancing?"

One kid from Texas got all the way to the na-
tional spelling bee finals and then lost the
prize. He couldn't spell "small."

The Eastern guest at a dude ranch watched
with fascination as the cowboy rolled a smoke.

"It's wonderful," he said to the cowboy,
"the way you roll that cigarette with just one
hand."

"Tain't nothin'," the cowboy replied. " 'T'
hardest part's gettin' the filter in."

One young man wanted to become a tree
surgeon, but he fainted at the sight of sap.

"Daddy," said the six-year-old, "before you
married Mommy, who told you how to drive?"

Someone ought to write a really modern Western. The big scene would feature the hero in front of the saloon trying to find a place for his horse.

Reruns of old movies on television are just another way of saying, "The evil men do oft lives after them."

The weather forecaster plotted his vacation with infinite care, even looking over the latest long-range photos from the weather satellites. He came back furious. "It rained every day of my vacation," he told his chief.

"You must be kidding," said the chief. "Where'd you get that magnificent suntan?"

"Suntan nothing," exploded the forecaster. "That's *rust!*"

In one Texas millionaire's home, the rugs are so thick that no one in the family has seen anyone below the neck for years.

A psychiatrist treated a patient for klepto-mania. After months of therapy the psychia-trist suggested the patient could consider him-self cured. "But if you have a relapse," cau-tioned the psychiatrist, "see if you can pick me up a small transistor radio."

One Hollywood star has been married so many times she has rice marks on her face.

The professional ballplayer was down on his luck. He was batting .150, he struck out three times in a row, he dropped the ball four times, and then he went down to the locker room to do a feature appearance in a shaving commer-cial and cut himself twice.

A teenager told her friend, "I hear the faculty is trying to stop necking in school."

The friend frowned and said, "Next thing you know, they'll be trying to make the stu-dents stop too."

If you didn't like seeing those teenagers at the drive-in restaurant combing their shoulder-length hair, remember that the girls are just as bad.

A Martian landed his saucer near a nightclub. Hearing the music, he sauntered into the club. Just then the drummer launched into a furious solo. The little green creature rushed up to the bandstand and whispered to the drum: "Need any help?"

Desperate girl to her last hope: "I like you just for what you are—alive!"

When a vacationer checked into an elegant resort hotel, the first room the manager showed him had a gold telephone, a hi-fi set, color television, a bar, and an indoor swimming pool. He was delighted. "I'll take it," he said.

"You can't," said the manager. "This is the elevator."

A woman never forgets her age . . . once she decides what it is.

Lady in an antique shop: "When I was here last week I saw a big mug with a flat head that holds a lot of beer. "I'd like to buy it."

Antique dealer: "I'm sorry, I can't sell it."

Lady. "Why not?"

Antique dealer: "That's my brother-in-law and he's just been drafted."

A television comedian who was running into low ratings decided to become a burglar, but he couldn't forget his old routine. After every robbery he'd stand in the doorway and say, "Thanks, all you lovely people, for letting me come into your living room tonight."

A banker never forgets he's a banker. You take one to lunch and ask him to pass the salt and he won't do it unless you pass him the pepper for security.

Grandfather says he recalls a farmer who was such a well-known liar that his wife had to call the hogs.

A soldier on leave walked into a recruiting office, sought out the recruiting sergeant, and whispered, "Would you mind giving me that sales talk again? I'm getting a little discouraged."

One sure way to know if you've had enough to drink is when somebody steps on your tongue.

There's something fresh and vital about living on a farm. Where else do you find people getting up to watch the Late Late show?

The Vice President mentioned recently that a woman might become President someday. But you have to be over 35 to be President, and where is there a woman who'll admit that she's over 35?

The freeways and turnpikes of America get more crowded every day. In New York a man started to get onto the freeway and a policeman stopped him. The man said, "What's the matter? Was I speeding?"

And the policeman said, "No, I just wanted to know if you have a reservation."

The saddest story is about a one-fingered pickpocket. All he could steal were Lifesavers.

If they draft women it'll be no problem to get them to fight—the sergeant will just have to yell "Charge!" and "Green Stamps!"

The husband was telling the neighbor that he got a dog for his wife, and it made the neigh-

bor mad because he couldn't make a trade like that.

Overheard from the next table: "I guess I wasn't too pretty when I was a baby. My parents had to buy me back from the dog catcher three times."

Psychiatrists tell us that one out of every four Americans is mentally ill. Check your friends. If three seem all right, you're the one.

Set in Intertype Walbaum at The Castle Press.
Typography by Grant Dahlstrom.
Printed on Hallmark Eggshell Book Paper.
Designed by Harald Peter.